Recht

*Enid Blyton's*

# Sleepytime
## TALES

For further information on Enid Blyton please visit www.blyton.com

ISBN 978-1-84135-529-0

First published by Award Publications Limited 2001
This edition first published 2007

Published by Award Publications Limited,
The Old Riding School, The Welbeck Estate,
Worksop, Nottinghamshire, S80 3LR

www.awardpublications.co.uk

3 5 7 9 10 8 6 4 2
10 12 14 16 18 20 19 17 15 13 11 09

Printed in China

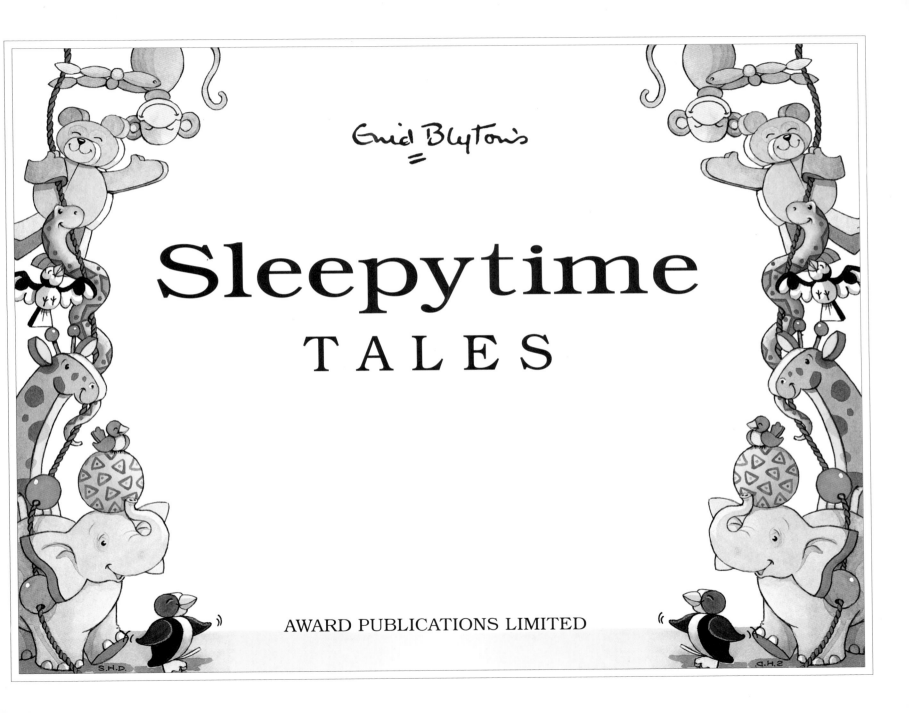

# Enid Blyton's

# Sleepytime
## TALES

AWARD PUBLICATIONS LIMITED

# The Stories

# 1

# The Enchanted Doll

Illustrated by Maggie Downer

Anna had a pretty doll called Victoria whom she loved very much indeed. The only thing she wished was that Victoria could walk and talk, instead of just lying or sitting perfectly still, staring at Anna with her wide-open blue eyes.

"I can pretend you talk to me, and I can pretend you run about and play," said Anna. "But you don't really and truly – and it *would* be such fun if just for once you would really come alive!"

Anna felt quite certain that if only she *could* walk and talk, she would make her a wonderful friend, for Anna had no brothers or sisters, so she was often lonely. That was why she played so much with Victoria. But Victoria just sat and stared, and didn't move a finger or say a word!

Then one day a very strange thing happened when Anna took Victoria for a walk in Pixie Wood. Although it had such a lovely name, Anna had never seen any pixies or anything at all exciting in Pixie Wood. It was just like an ordinary wood.

But today it seemed a little different. The trees seemed closer together, as if they were nodding and whispering to one another. The sun couldn't get in between the branches, and the wood was dark and rather mysterious. Anna took Victoria by the hand and walked her over the grass, talking to her. Her doll's pram was broken and had gone to be mended, which was why Victoria was not riding in it as usual.

Anna walked on through the wood and then stopped suddenly in surprise. In front of her stood a tiny pram, a little smaller than a doll's pram, and it shone like pure gold. It had a little white hood with a silver fringe, and the pram cover was white too, with gold embroidery on it.

"Whatever is a doll's pram doing here?" wondered Anna, for she knew there were no other children about.

Anna went over to the pram and turned back the cover. There was no doll inside – but would you believe it, there was a little bottle full of milk!

"But this pram can't belong to a *real* baby!" cried Anna in astonishment. "It's far too small. Oh! Goodness me! It might belong to a pixie baby!"

Anna waited for a little while to see if anyone came, but nobody did. Then she began to wonder. Would it matter if she wheeled Victoria about in the pram for five minutes? Surely it would do no harm. So Anna picked up her doll and strapped her in. She set the soft pillow up behind her so that she could sit up comfortably and tucked the white cover round her legs.

But as she was about to wheel her around the little wood, Anna thought she saw a little pointed face peeping at her from behind a tree.

"Who's there?" she called. There was no answer – so Anna left the pram and ran to the tree to see if there really was a pixie peeping there. But there was no one at all except a scurrying rabbit with a white bobtail!

Anna turned back and was amazed to see the pram running away! It was wheeling off all by itself, between the trees, as fast as ever it could!

"Come back, come back!" shouted Anna. "Oh, please, pram, do come back! Don't take Victoria away!" She ran after the pram as fast as she could, shouting as she went. The pram went faster and faster. It turned a corner by some thick bushes, and disappeared from sight.

Anna ran wildly about, and began to cry when she could not see the pram anywhere.

"Where have you gone, Victoria?" she shouted.

But there was no answer. Victoria had disappeared with the pram. Anna sat down and cried bitterly.

Presently she felt a little hand on her shoulder and a high, twittering voice said: "What's the matter? Would you mind getting up? You are sitting on my front door."

Anna looked up in surprise. A tiny creature with long, pointed wings, pointed ears, and pointed shoes stood beside her.

"Are you a pixie?" asked Anna, in astonishment. "Am I really sitting on your front door? I'm so sorry." She got up, and saw that she was sitting on a small yellow trap door, half hidden by fallen leaves.

"Why are you crying?" the pixie asked.

Anna told him all about the little pram she had found, and how it had run off with her doll.

"Oh, that pram belongs to Mother Dimity, the Old Woman Who Lives In A Shoe," said the pixie. "She is very forgetful, you know, and leaves it about everywhere! If she goes home without it, all she has to do is whistle for it and it will run home on its own."

"Well, it's taken my doll too," said Anna, beginning to cry again.

"Please don't do that," said the pixie. "You are making my home all damp. Anyway, you can easily find your doll. Mother Dimity will give her back if you ask her nicely."

"But where does she live?" asked Anna.

"Why, in the Shoe of course," said the pixie. "Knock at the Big Oak Tree six times, go down the steps and find a boat to take you on the Underground River. Then ask the Wizard Who Grows Toadstools where the Shoe is. He is sure to know, because the Old Woman is his sister."

"Thank you," said Anna, getting up. The pixie said goodbye and shut his trapdoor with a bang, leaving Anna to look for the Big Oak Tree.

Anna soon found a large oak tree. She knocked
on it, but nothing happened. Then she saw
the biggest oak tree she had ever seen in
her life!

"That's the one!" thought Anna, and
she ran over to it. She knocked on
the trunk sharply six times –
rat-tat-tat-tat-tat-tat! Then there
came a creaking noise, and to
her delight a small door
swung open in the tree.
A narrow flight of steps
led downwards
through the roots.

Anna slipped through the door, which at once shut with a bang, and began to go down the steps. It was rather dark, but small lanterns hung here and there giving a little light. Anna climbed down a long way.

Eventually she came to a wide passage, with a row of doors on each side. She looked closely at them. Each door had a name on it , or a message, written on a little white card.

The first card said: "Please ring, don't knock." The second said: "Please knock, don't ring." And the third door had a card that said: "Please don't knock or ring." As if that wasn't enough, the fourth door said: "I am not at home yesterday or tomorrow."

Anna thought that was very strange, and she giggled. The doors also had names on them and they were strange too.

"Mister Woozle" was on one card, and "Dame High-come-quick" was on another. Anna decided to walk straight on, and at last she heard the sound of lapping water.

"That must be the Underground River," she thought, pleased. "Now I must find a boat!"

She soon came to the riverbank. It was hung with fairy lights of all colours and looked very pretty. There were plenty of boats on the side of it, but none of them had oars. Anna looked about for someone to row her down the river, but she could see no one.

"Is there anyone here?" she shouted. Then a furry head came poking out of a funny little ticket-office that Anna had not noticed.

"Yes, I'm here, and you're here too," said the voice from the ticket office. Anna went up and saw a grey rabbit with a collar round its neck, and a spotty tie, very neatly knotted.

"Good morning," said Anna. "I would like to borrow a boat."

"Here's your ticket, then," said the friendly rabbit, handing her a very chewed-looking piece of cardboard.

"How much is it?" asked Anna.

"Oh, nothing!" he replied cheerily. "Everything is free here!"

"Where's the boatman?" asked Anna.

"Nowhere," said the rabbit. "There isn't one."

"Then how can I go anywhere?" asked Anna.

"Climb in," said the rabbit, "and the boat will take you."

Anna frowned at the rabbit, and walked up to one of the boats. She chose a blue one, dotted with gold stars, and climbed into it. At once the boat set off by itself.

It shot on down the river, and after a little while it left the underground tunnel and came out into the open air. The boat sped on and on, and Anna saw with surprise that the surrounding fields were full of animals dressed up like human beings.

Suddenly Anna saw a curious sight. In the middle of a field stood a strange-looking old man waving a stick about. He was surrounded by toadstools of all sizes, colours and shapes, and she guessed that he must be the Wizard Who Grows Toadstools.

"Stop, stop!" she cried to the boat. It stopped at once and headed towards the bank. Anna patted the boat, said thank you and then jumped out. She went up to the old wizard. He didn't see her at first and almost knocked her over with his silver wand.

"Please," she said. "I've come to ask you where your sister, the Old Woman Who Lives In A Shoe, is. I want to go and speak to her."

"You'll find her on the other side of that hill," said the wizard, waving his wand violently. "Look out! You are standing just where my next toadstool is growing!"

Just then Anna felt the earth
pushing up under her feet.
A big toadstool appeared
right beneath her. It was
covered with big red
spots.

"Thank you," said Anna and ran out of the field as quickly as she could. She made her way to the hill in the distance. She climbed it, and as soon as she came to the top she saw the Shoe.

It was enormous, and it had windows and doors and a chimney at the top. Anna thought it looked lovely. She ran down to it, and at once she was surrounded by a crowd of small pixie children, with pointed faces, pointed ears and short wings.

"Who are you? Where do you come from?" they cried in excitement. "Have you come to see our new child?"

"You can see her through the window!" said a tiny pixie, taking Anna's hand and leading her to a window. Anna peeped in – and there, in the bed nearest the window, lay Victoria, her very own doll!

"She arrived today in Mother Dimity's pram," explained the pixie. "But she won't talk, or eat, or drink. She won't even blink her eyes!"

"That's because she isn't a little girl at all," cried Anna. "She's my doll and her name is Victoria!"

"A doll!" said the pixie children, crowding round Anna. "What's a doll? We don't know what a doll is."

"Well, a doll is – a doll is – well, that's what a doll is!" said Anna, pointing to where Victoria lay on the little bed.

"But can't the poor thing move or talk at all?" asked the pixies in surprise.

"Of course not," said Anna and she ran in through the door of the big Shoe, and bumped into the Old Woman.

"Now then, gently, gently!" said Mother Dimity. "You'll frighten the new little girl, rushing about like that. I've just given her some very strong magic medicine to make her come alive again."

"She never has been alive!" cried Anna. "She's my doll!"

"Your doll!" said the Old Woman. "Oh goodness! I remember once seeing a doll in the Land of Boys and Girls. Well, she looks a lot like a little girl, don't you agree? And she'll be even more like one now that I've given her the medicine."

"Do you mean to say that Victoria will be able to walk and talk?" cried Anna.

"Of course," said Mother Dimity. "Look – she is blinking her eyes now! Perhaps I had better change her back into a doll again."

"No, please don't," said Anna at once. She ran to Victoria and looked at her. The little doll was opening and shutting her eyes and she suddenly looked at Anna and smiled a wide smile, showing all her pretty teeth.

"Hello," she said. "I've often wanted to talk to you, and now I can!"

"Oh, what fun we'll have together now!" Anna cried, hugging her doll to her. "We can talk to one another, and play all kinds of games."

"But you mustn't let any one but yourself know," said Mother Dimity at once. "If you do, the magic will disappear, and Victoria will be an ordinary doll again."

"Oh, I won't tell any one at all!" said Anna, happily. "Come on, Victoria, we'll go home now. It must be getting late."

Mother Dimity showed them a quick way home, and they arrived there just in time for dinner. Anna put Victoria in her cot, and told her to be sure not to move if any one came in, and she promised. And now Anna is as happy as can be, for she has a real, live doll to play with her, and they *do* have some fine games together.

"Really!" Anna's mother often says, "you might think that doll was alive, the way Anna plays with her all day long!"

And then Anna smiles a big smile – but she doesn't say a word! She has a wonderful secret to keep and she keeps it very well!

# 2

# Lion
# Learns a Lesson

Illustrated by Sue Deakin

Sophie had a big Noah's Ark.
It was a splendid one, and
as well as Noah's family,
there were two of every
animal you can think of!

Lions, tigers, bears, horses, pandas,
dogs, giraffes, elephants, ducks,
chickens, pigs – there didn't
seem to be any animal that
wasn't there!

Sophie enjoyed playing with her ark. Every day she set the animals out in twos and made them walk into the ark with Mr. and Mrs. Noah. They liked this very much.

But at night the Noah's Ark animals had
even better fun! Mr. Noah opened the door
of the ark and let them all out to play!

They all tumbled out on to the ground and played whatever game they liked best. The ducks and hens played hide-and-seek, the giraffes played at racing, the elephants drew pictures, and the bears played leap frog. Mr. and Mrs. Noah and Shem, Ham and Japheth, their three sons, watched them and laughed.

When it was time for all the animals to go back into the ark they lined up in twos and marched in quietly. Then Mr. Noah shut the door after them and they all lay quietly in the ark without moving, waiting for the time to come when Sophie would open the lid and take them out.

Now all the animals were very good except the lion. He thought a great deal of himself ever since he had heard Sophie call him the king of the beasts. He wandered off each night by himself, for he thought he was too grand to play games with the others.

He sat by the fire and curled his long tail round him. Sometimes he nibbled a bit of the hearthrug. Sometimes he climbed up to the clock on the bookshelf and listened to its funny, ticking voice.

And when he heard Mr. Noah calling all the animals back into the ark, the lion turned up his nose and stayed where he was! *He* didn't want to go inside. Wasn't he the king of all the beasts? Why should he be hustled into the ark like the stupid ducks and hens and pigs?

Mr. Noah got very cross with the lion.

"Where's that lion tonight?" he would say. "He is just too tiresome for anything! Lion, lion, come at once! The other animals are all ready to march into the ark, and your lioness is waiting. Come at once."

But usually Shem had to go and find him and drag him to the ark. It was a great nuisance because it kept all the other animals waiting.

Now this happened night after night, and Mr. Noah got very tired of it.

"If you don't come when you're called tonight, lion, we shall march into the ark without you, and you will be shut out!" he said firmly.

"They won't dare to go without me," thought the lion to himself. "I shall keep them waiting as long as I please! Am I not the king of them all?"

That night he sat himself down
by the warm fire, curled his tail
round him like a cat, and looked
down his nose at the bears
playing blind man's
buff nearby.

When the time came, Mr. Noah
called to the animals.
"Come to the ark! Line up
in twos!" he cried. "It is time
to go back."

All the animals and birds at once stopped their play and ran to the ark. The kangaroos were first. They stood at the front of the line, and after them came lots of other animals – the pandas, and then the brown bears, and then the pigs, and then, all by herself, the lioness. The lion was missing as usual. The line stretched out in twos, past the monkeys and elephants, and ended with the tigers, who had been playing hide-and-seek, and had had to scramble out of the coal scuttle to get to the ark.

Mr. Noah saw that the lion was missing, but he said nothing. He didn't even look round to see where the lion was. He didn't tell Shem to go and get him. He just said,

"Shem, open the door. Ham, see that the elephants don't tread on the pigs. Japheth, tell the dogs to stop barking. Mrs. Noah, please would you be good enough to lead the way in?"

Mrs. Noah led the way. The animals went in two by two, except the lioness, who went in by herself. Mr. Noah went in last. He shut the door with a bang. Soon all the animals had settled down in the ark. Not a sound was to be heard.

Now the lion was rather astonished to see that all the animals had gone in without him. But he didn't say a word or even move from the hearthrug where he sat warming himself.

"I shall stay out as long as I like," he said to himself grandly. He looked round and saw that all the other toys were going into the toy cupboard. The dolls and the teddy bear always came out to play at night too. But now they were settling down quietly.

The teddy bear was surprised to see the lion on the hearthrug. "Aren't you going to get into the ark?" he asked. "Won't you be frightened out here all alone?"

"Frightened!" said the lion, turning up his nose. "*Frightened!* Don't you know I am the king of all the beasts, and as brave as can be? What should frighten *me* I should like to know?"

"Well, if you feel as grand as all that, you can do what you like!" said the teddy bear in a huff. "I'm sure I don't care, Mr. High-and-Mighty!"

He went into the toy cupboard
and slammed the door. The
lion was now all alone. He
sat on the rug and blinked
at the fire. It would soon
be out. The nursery was
dark, but the lion could
see quite well. He had
eyes like a cat.

He sat there, and he sat there. Suddenly he heard a scratching noise in the wall nearby. He jumped to his feet. Whatever could it be?

It was the little brown mouse who lived behind the wall. He was coming out of his hole to see if the children had left any crumbs on the floor. He sidled out of the hole and ran over the hearthrug. He bumped into the lion and trod on his long tail.

"Ouch!" said the lion. "Why don't you look where you're going!" The mouse stared at him and grinned. He ran at the lion and bumped into him again.

"I am the king of the beasts!" said the lion in his grandest voice. "So you'd better not do that again!"

"Well, you're sitting on a crumb," said the mouse. "And I want to eat it."

The lion sat down on the crumb and wouldn't move. He felt very angry with the mouse.

"I wonder if *you* are good to eat!" said the mouse suddenly. "Do you mind if I nibble your tail?"

"Yes, I do mind," said the lion who was suddenly scared. The mouse tried to get the lion's tail in his mouth and the lion ran away. The mouse chased him. He thought it was fun!

"I'll catch you in a minute!" squeaked the mouse. "And then I'll bite your tail!"

This frightened the lion even more. He ran to the ark and knocked loudly on the door.

"Let me in!" he cried. "A mouse is chasing me."

"The door is locked," said Mr. Noah. "And we are all in bed."

The lion ran to the toy cupboard, and knocked there.

"Let me in!" he cried. "A mouse is chasing me!"

"Go away," said the teddy bear sleepily. "You're waking us up."

Well, the lion would certainly have had his tail nibbled if someone hadn't come into the nursery on velvet paws and scared the mouse away. And that someone was the big tabby cat! She had smelt the mouse and had come after it.

The mouse shot into his hole. Then the cat saw the lion running and thought he must be a mouse too. So she went after him, and at last she caught him. She pushed him over and sniffed at him. He was very frightened. He felt sure she would eat him.

"You smell strange," said the cat. "Very strange indeed. You smell of wood and paint. I will not eat you – but I will play with you."

She began to push the poor lion
about and throw him up into
the air. He ran away as fast
as he could and once
more banged at the
door of the ark.

"Let me in, let me in!" he cried. "A cat is after me."

"The door is locked," said Mr. Noah. "We don't want to be woken up."

Then the lion ran to the toy cupboard and knocked again.

"Please let me in!" he cried. "A cat is after me."

"Go away," said the teddy bear sleepily. "Do not wake us."

The poor lion did not know what to do – and then he suddenly saw the cat running out of the nursery door. She had heard a mouse downstairs and had gone to chase it.

The lion sat down in front of the fire again, tired and miserable. How he wished he was safely in the ark with all the other animals!

As he sat there a big spider ran over the rug and made him jump!

"Whatever's this now!" cried the lion. "Go away, whatever you are!"

"I'm going to spin a web from your nose to the leg of the chair," said the spider. "Keep still!"

The lion gave a howl and ran away. He knew it was no use going to the ark. He knew it was no use going to the toy cupboard either. Where could he go to hide from all the mice, and cats, and spiders?

"What about the dolls' house?" he thought to himself. He ran over to it and pushed the front door. It opened!

The lion slipped inside, shut the door and went into the kitchen. He sat down in a chair there and sighed. At last he was safe!

He didn't feel brave now. And he didn't feel at all like the king of the beasts. He just felt like a very small and lonely and frightened lion.

The next morning Sophie found the lion in the dolls' house, and *how* surprised she was!

"How did he get there?" she wondered as she put him back into the ark. And that night, when the animals clambered out of the ark, the lion went too… but he didn't go and sit on the hearthrug alone, looking haughty and grand.

No, he mixed with the others and played tag and hide-and-seek! And when Mr. Noah called the animals to him, who was the first one to come? Yes – the lion! He wasn't going to be locked out again! He had had enough of being grand and mighty. He just wanted to play with the bears and go into the ark with all the others.

The lioness teases him sometimes. She says,

"Who spent the night in the dolls' house like a doll? And who got chased by a mouse, and a cat, and a spider?" And do you know, the lion just goes red and doesn't say a word!

# 3

# Billy and
# the West Wind

Illustrated by Maggie Downer

Billy's mother was very unhappy. When Billy came home from school she had tears in her eyes and she was hunting all over the place for something.

"What's the matter, Mummy?" asked Billy in surprise, for he thought that grown-ups never cried.

"I've lost my lovely diamond ring," said his mother. "It's the one your daddy gave me years ago, and I love it best of all my rings. It was loose and it must have dropped off. Now I can't find it anywhere, and I'm so unhappy about it."

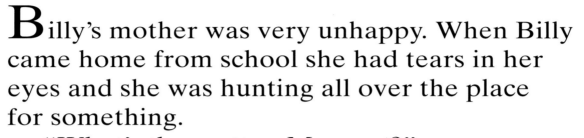

"I'll help you to look for it," said
Billy, at once. "Just tell me all the
places you've been this morning,
Mummy."

"I had it on at breakfast-time,"
said his mother. "Then I went
to see old Mrs. Brown who
lives at the far edge of the
meadow. I may have
dropped it on my way
there, of course.
Perhaps you'd like
to go and look on
the path, Billy."

So off Billy ran, his eyes looking all over the ground as he went. It was very windy, and the grass kept blowing about, which made it very difficult to see the ground properly. He soon came to the meadow and then he went down on his hands and knees and began to look very carefully indeed. He did so want to find that ring!

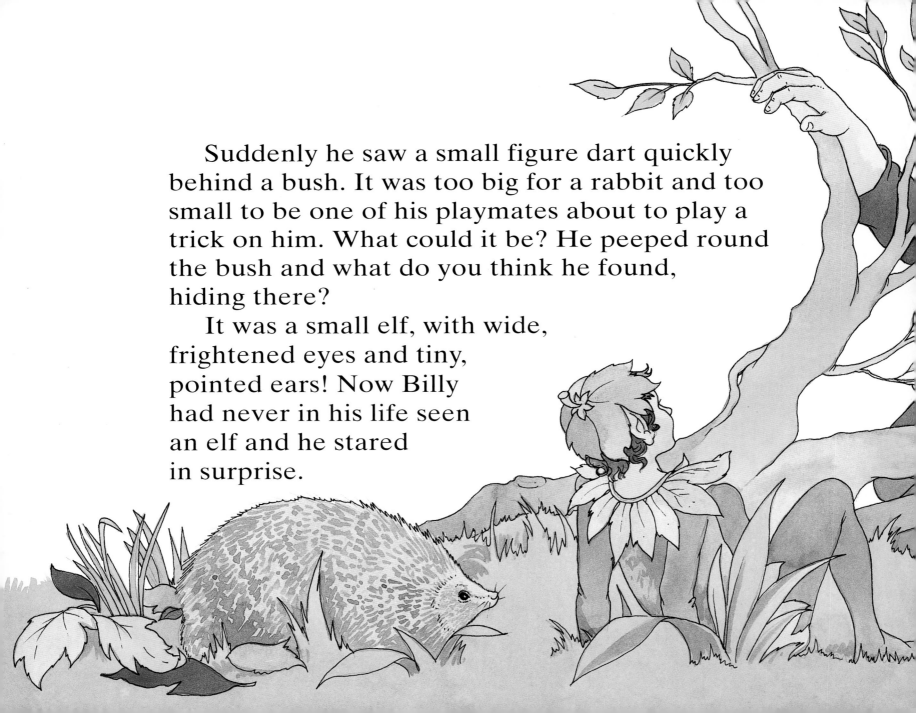

Suddenly he saw a small figure dart quickly behind a bush. It was too big for a rabbit and too small to be one of his playmates about to play a trick on him. What could it be? He peeped round the bush and what do you think he found, hiding there?

It was a small elf, with wide, frightened eyes and tiny, pointed ears! Now Billy had never in his life seen an elf and he stared in surprise.

"Please don't hurt me!"
said the elf, in a little
tinkling voice.
"Of course I won't!"
said Billy. "But where
are your wings? I
thought all elves had
wings and could fly."

"Well, I usually *do* have wings," said the little creature who was clothed in a beautiful suit of purple and blue. "They are lovely silver ones, and I took them off this morning to clean them. I put them down on that bush there, and the wind came along and blew them away. Now I'm looking everywhere for them, but I can't find them anywhere. It's too awful!"

"I'm looking for something too," said Billy. "I'm hunting for my mother's diamond ring. Have you seen it?"

"No," said the elf. "But I can easily get it for you, if you'll help me find my wings."

"Could you really?" said Billy, excitedly. "But how am I to help *you*?"

"You could go to the West Wind and ask him what he's done with my wings," said the elf. "I can't do it myself because I'm afraid of him – he's so big and blustery – but you are big and tall so perhaps you wouldn't mind."

"What an adventure this is turning out to be!" thought Billy to himself, feeling more and more excited.

"Of course I will help you," said Billy to the elf. "But wherever will I find the West Wind? I didn't even know it was a person!"

"Oh, goodness!" said the elf, laughing. "He's very much a person, I can tell you. He's gone to see his cousin, the Rainbow Lady, on the top of Blowaway Hill."

"Where's that?" asked Billy. "Tell me, and I'll go straight away."

"Well, the quickest way is to find the tower in the wood," said the elf, pointing down a little rabbit-path through some trees. "It has two doors. Go in the one that faces the sun. Shut it. Wish that you could be in the same place as the West Wind. Open the other door and you'll find yourself there! Then just ask the West Wind what he's done with my wings and tell him he really must let me have them back."

Billy waved goodbye and ran off down the narrow little path. He had never been down it before. After a while he came to a tall, thin tower amongst the trees. Billy walked all round it. It looked very strange indeed. There were no windows, but there were two small round doors. One faced the sun and the other was in shadow, just as the elf had described.

Billy opened the sunny door and walked boldly through. The tower was high, dark, and cold inside. Shivering, Billy shut the door behind him and found himself in black darkness, just like night! He felt a little frightened, but he remembered what the elf had said and shouted:

"I wish I was on the top of Blowaway Hill."

He heard a faint rushing sound and the tower rocked very slightly. Billy opened the other door and daylight streamed into the strange tower, making him blink. He walked out of the door – and *how* surprised he was!

He was no longer in the wood – he was on the top of a sunny hill, and in front of him was a small pretty cottage, overgrown with honeysuckle.

"This must be the Rainbow Lady's house," thought Billy. He marched up the little path and knocked at the door. A voice called "Come in!" So Billy turned the handle...

A draught of cold air blew on him as soon as he stepped inside. He shivered and looked round in surprise. Two people were sitting drinking lemonade at a little round table. A fire burned brightly in one corner and a grey cat sat washing itself on the rug. Everything seemed quite ordinary until he looked at the people there!

One was the Rainbow Lady. She was very beautiful and her dress was so bright that Billy blinked his eyes when he looked at her. She was dressed in all the colours of the rainbow, and her dress floated out around her like a mist. Her eyes shone like two stars.

The other person was the West Wind. He was fat and blustery, and his breath came in great gusts as if he had been running very hard. It was his breathing that made the big windy draughts that blew round the little room. His clothes were like April clouds and blew out round him all the time. Billy was so astonished to see him that at first he couldn't say a word.

"Well! What do you want?" asked the West Wind in a gusty voice. As he spoke Billy felt a shower of raindrops fall on him. It was very strange.

"I've come from the little elf who lives down in the meadow," said Billy. "She says you took away her wings this morning, West Wind, and she does so badly want them back."

"Dear me!" said the West Wind, surprised, and as he spoke another shower of raindrops fell on Billy's head. "How was I to know they belonged to the elf? I thought they had been put there by someone who didn't want them! I knew the red goblin was wanting a pair of wings so I blew them to him!"

"Oh dear!" said Billy, in dismay. "What a pity! The elf is really very upset. She can't fly, you see. She only took them off to clean them."

"West Wind, you are always doing silly things like that," said the Rainbow Lady, in a soft voice. "One day you will get into trouble. You had better go to the red goblin and ask for those wings back."

"Oh, no, I can't do that," said the West Wind, looking very uncomfortable and puffing more raindrops all over the room.

Billy looked round to see if there was an umbrella anywhere. It was not very nice to have showers of rain falling all over him whenever the West Wind spoke. He found an umbrella in a corner and put it up over himself.

"Oh, yes, you *can* go and get the wings back," said the Rainbow Lady, and she said it so firmly that the West Wind eventually agreed. He got up, took Billy's hand and went sulkily out of the door. He had a very cold, wet hand, but Billy didn't mind. It was very exciting.

The West Wind took Billy down the hill at such a pace that the little boy gasped for breath. They came to a river and the Wind jumped straight across it, dragging Billy with him. Then he rushed across some fields and at last came to a small, lop-sided house. A tiny goblin sat in the garden with a schoolbook, crying bitterly. The West Wind took no notice of the little creature but walked quickly up and knocked on the door.

"Stay here," he said to Billy, and left him in the garden. The little boy went over to the goblin.

"What's the matter?" he asked. The little goblin looked up. He had a quaint, pointed face and different coloured eyes – one was green and the other was yellow.

"I can't do my homework," he said. "Look! It's taking-away sums and this one *won't* take away."

Billy looked – and then he smiled – for the silly little goblin had put the sum down wrong! He had to take 18 from 81, and he had written the sum upside down so that he was trying to take 81 away from 18. No wonder it wouldn't come right!

Billy put the sum down right for him and the goblin did it easily. He was *so* grateful.

"Is there anything else I can help you with?" asked Billy kindly.

"Well," said the goblin shyly. "I never can remember which is my right hand and which is my left, and I'm always getting into dreadful trouble at school because of that. I suppose you can't tell me the best way to remember which hand is which?"

"Oh, that's easy!" said Billy at once. "The hand you are *writing* with is your *right* hand, and the one that's *left* is the *left* one, of course!"

"Oh, that's wonderful!" said the little goblin, in delight. "I shall never forget now. I always know which hand I write with, so I shall always know my *right* hand and the other one *must* be the left. Right hand, left hand, right hand, left hand!"

Just at that moment the door of the little house flew open and out came the West Wind in a fearful temper.

"That miserable red goblin won't give me back those wings!" he roared, and a whole shower of rain fell heavily on poor Billy and his new goblin friend. "So we can't have them!"

Billy stared in dismay. Now he wouldn't be able to take them to the elf and she wouldn't give him his mother's ring! It was too bad. He looked so upset that the small goblin he had just helped gently took hold of his hand.

"What's the matter?" he asked. "Do you want those silver wings that the West Wind gave my father this morning? They were really for me to learn to fly on, but if you badly want them, you shall have them back. You've been so kind to me! I'd like to do something in return!"

"Oh, *would* you let me have the wings!" said Billy, in delight. The little goblin said nothing but ran indoors. He came out with a pair of glittering silver wings and gave them to Billy. The little boy thanked him joyfully and turned to go. The West Wind took his hand and back they went to Blowaway Hill again.

"Well, you never know when a little kindness is going to bring you a big reward!" said the West Wind, in a jolly voice. "It's a good thing you helped that little goblin, isn't it?"

"Oh, yes," said Billy happily. "Now I must get back to the meadow again and give these wings to the elf."

But when he turned to look, he was dismayed to see that the tower had disappeared.

"Oh no!" he cried. "The tower has gone! However am I to get back home?"

Poor Billy! It was quite true – the magic tower had gone and could not take him back to the wood as he had planned! But luckily the Rainbow Lady was watching through the window and came out to see what was wrong.

"Don't worry," she said when Billy explained what had happened. "Just put on these elf wings, and the West Wind will blow you gently through the air back to the meadow."

The Rainbow Lady took the wings from Billy and clipped them neatly on to his shoulders.

"Now!" she said, turning to the West Wind. "I said GENTLY, so please don't be rough. Remember your manners for once!"

Then Billy felt himself rising into the air, higher and higher until he was far above the hill. His wings beat gently backwards and forwards and the West Wind blew him swiftly along. It was a most wonderful feeling.

"This is the most marvellous adventure I shall ever have!" said Billy, joyfully. "Oh, how I wish I always had wings! It is lovely to fly like this!"

The West Wind smiled and remembered his manners and did not blow too roughly. Soon Billy could see the meadow far below and the two of them started to glide gently downwards.

The West Wind said goodbye and left Billy on the edge of wood. He soon found a path he knew and ran along to the bush where he had seen the elf. She was still there waiting for him. When she saw that he had her wings on his back she cried out in delight and ran to meet him.

She unclipped her wings
from Billy's shoulders
and put them on her own.
"Oh, thank you, thank
you!" she cried.

"Could you give me my
mother's ring now?"
asked Billy. "You said you
would if I helped you."

"Of course!" said the elf. "Whilst you were gone I set all the rabbits in the wood hunting for me – and one of them brought me this lovely shining ring. Is it your mother's?"

Of course, it was! So Billy ran all the way home and when he showed his mother the ring she could hardly believe her eyes.

"You *are* clever to find it!" she said.

"I didn't find it – a rabbit found it," said Billy. But his mother didn't believe him, and when he told her his adventure she said he really must have been dreaming!

So next week he is going to ask that elf to come to tea with him – and then everyone will know it wasn't a dream! I wish I was going for tea with them, too, don't you?